Vera Wang

Queen of Fashion

Amazing Chinese American

by Ai-Ling Louie

illustrated by Cathy Peng

dragoneagle press

Imagine growing up like a princess. That's what Chinese American Vera Wang's childhood was like. Vera came from a very wealthy family. She lived in the best places in New York City. She never had to work for a living, but she did!

Vera is now a top fashion designer. She works very hard. She works day and night to make sure her company is successful. How did this princess become a hard-working businesswoman? It wasn't easy!

Vera's parents, C.C. and Florence, came to the United
States from China. It was the 1940's. Only 105 Chinese
people a year were allowed to come to the United States.
A man who came from England or France could bring his
family to America. A Chinese workingman could not.
The American government did not want too many Chinese.
It was a time of discrimination.

C.C. and Florence were lucky. They had rich important families. They helped them enter the United States as a family.

C.C. was a businessman. His company bought things all over the world and sold them in the U.S. He and Florence lived on the Upper East Side of New York City. The Upper East Side had handsome wide streets. Some of the richest people in America had homes there. The Wangs were one of the only Chinese families.

Vera was born in 1949. She was Florence and C.C.'s first child. Florence loved to dress Vera and her younger brother Kenneth. Florence bought them very fine clothes. Sometimes people turned to look at them when they walked down the street. New Yorkers were not used to seeing Chinese children.

Florence bought some of her own clothes from Europe. She took her young daughter to the fashion shows in France. Florence and Vera would sit by the runway. The most famous designers in the world showed their amazing creations.

One Christmas morning, Vera opened a big box. Inside she found a pair of ice skates. C.C. promised to take Vera to Central Park to try them out.

The cold nipped Vera's nose. She didn't care.
She watched the skaters twirl and leap. It looked as
if they were dancing on air. Vera walked onto the ice.
Down she went! It wasn't as easy as it looked.

Vera learned the beautiful skaters had taken lessons.
She wanted to take skating lessons too. "Maybe…" said
her father. Vera asked again and again. She was not
going to forget about her wish.
Finally, her father said yes.

Vera started skating lessons when she was seven. She woke up early to go to her six o'clock skating lesson. She went to a private school for girls. After school, she returned to the rink for practice. She also took ballet lessons to help her become a more graceful skater. Vera did her homework in the evening. She was exhausted by the time she fell into bed.

Vera kept up her busy schedule all through her school years. She loved skating! She loved dancing to the music. She loved getting a new dress for every contest. Vera began making little drawings of skating costumes. She showed them to her mother. "That one will show off your long legs," Florence said.

"Will it flip around when I do my jumps?" Vera asked.

"Only if we use something lightweight. And we'll have it cut a special way," Florence answered.

Florence and Vera decided on a costume together. Florence watched carefully as the dressmaker fitted the costume on her daughter.

Vera dreamed of entering the biggest skating contest of all. She wanted to represent the United States at the Olympics. Vera and her coaches, Sonya and Peter Dunfield, decided Vera should enter in pairs competitions. They chose a boy named James Stuart as Vera's partner. He was tall and dark. He and Vera looked good together.

Vera and James entered a lot of contests before
the 1968 Olympics. They had to do well in every one.
The first was the North Atlantic contest.

Vera had just started college. She wanted to skate.
Her father wanted her to become a doctor. So that is
what Vera studied to be. She had to work and study

long hard hours. Her coach Sonya said, "I don't know how she does it all!" But Vera was showing that lots of work didn't scare her.

She and James won the North Atlantic contest.
They won a silver medal in their next competition, the
Eastern Regionals. That was good enough for them to
go on to the National title competition.

Vera and James got dressed in their specially designed costumes. Their families hugged them and wished them luck. Sonya and Peter gave them last words of advice. They were almost to their dream. The Olympics were within their reach. Vera tried to quiet her nerves and steady her breathing. They glided across the ice and James lifted her high into the air.

But it wasn't good enough. She and James came in sixth place. There would be no Olympics for Vera.

Vera says, "I was devastated!" The dream was gone. The princess had lost the one thing she wanted most.

Vera felt terrible. She couldn't concentrate on her schoolwork. She left college. She had to figure things out.

It took a long time. What should she do with her life? She had always liked drawing her skating costumes. She decided to study art. She returned to college and graduated.

Vera told her mother and father she wanted to become a fashion designer. Her father thought it was a very risky business. He thought it was wrong for his daughter. He would not pay for her to attend fashion school. But Vera knew what she wanted.

She went to work for *Vogue Magazine*. It was an important magazine for women's fashion. At *Vogue* she could learn about the fashion business. Vera did whatever needed to be done in the office. She made photocopies. She brought the clothes in for models to wear. When Vera had a good idea, she spoke up. People listened. They liked what she had to say. Vera was made the youngest Fashion Editor at *Vogue*. She was twenty-three.

A fashion editor decides how to photograph the new
designer clothes. Once, Vera had the idea of showing
model Christie Brinkley walking some dogs. She chose
Dobermans, who are very fierce. She thought it would be
like Beauty and the Beasts. It was almost too much
like that. One of the dogs tried to bite Christie's leg!

Vera was such a hard-worker that people around the office began to call her Miss *Vogue*. She worked there for sixteen years.

While she was working for *Vogue*, Vera met Arthur Becker. He was a businessman. They were in Hawaii when he asked her to marry him.

Vera wanted a big wedding. People from the fashion world would be invited. Her relatives would come all the way from Hong Kong. Vera had to have a very special dress. She looked all over. She tried on dress after dress. They were all so frilly. Vera wanted something simple and elegant. Vera's wedding gown was beaded lace. It weighed fourteen pounds. She hated it. Luckily, in Chinese custom the bride changes to a different dress for the reception. Vera put on a silk slip dress for her entry into the grand ballroom. There she danced for the first time with her new husband, Arthur.

Vera got a job designing hats, purses and shoes for Ralph Lauren. She and Arthur couldn't wait to start a family. They adopted a baby girl, Josephine, in 1990. They adopted Cecilia in 1993.

Vera's father had been watching her career very carefully. He had come to respect her success in the fashion world. He offered to help her start her own fashion business. He gave her four million dollars. At long last, she was going to have the chance to be a fashion designer.

Vera opened a bridal shop in New York City. She wanted to help other brides find dresses for their wedding. Vera designed bridal gowns for the modern woman. Vera's gowns didn't have a lot of decoration.

They were simple and elegant. More and more brides came to the Vera Wang Bridal Shop. But Vera was still losing money. She had to do something fast.

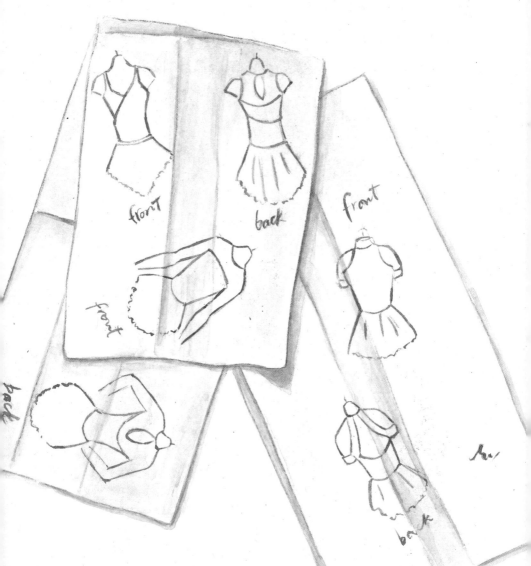

In 1994 Vera got a chance to design a skating dress.
It was for Olympic-skater Nancy Kerrigan. Vera used
everything she had learned from her own skating days.
She covered Nancy's dress with tiny mirrors. When she
glided over the ice, Nancy sparkled like a star. Nancy
won the Silver Medal at the Olympics that year. Vera's

dress was shown over and over on television. It was in lots of magazines. It was in every newspaper. Everyone wanted to know who designed such a perfect dress?

It was a big break for
Vera. She wasn't just a bridal
designer anymore. Movie stars
wore her dresses to the Oscars.
Her name appeared on Vera
Wang Perfume and Vera Wang
Fine China and Glassware.

Today, Vera is sitting by the runway once again. This time it's her runway. She is rehearsing models to show off the clothes she has just designed. It's Vera Wang's Spring Collection. And you can bet it will be a big success!

The Vera Wang Company is a three hundred million dollar business. It gives jobs to hundreds of people. Vera's name is known worldwide. She does very important work. She loves every minute!

Vera stood before a cheering crowd of the top people in United States fashion. She won the award of 2005 Womenswear Designer of the Year. She was fifty-five years old. She had worked long and hard. She was no longer a princess. She was Queen of the American Fashion World. There was a big smile on her face. Her arms were around her two young daughters. She told everyone, "Look at me--even at my age, dreams do come true!"

Notes On Chinese American Immigration

In 1965, when Vera was sixteen, the Immigration and
Nationality Act was signed. The new Act stopped the unfair
system of letting in more Europeans than people from Asia.
Discrimination against the Chinese was no longer the law
of the land. Many Chinese Americans had worked to change
the laws. Today Chinese children can come to America.
In 1950, there were only twenty thousand Chinese in New York
City and almost all of these were single men. By the year 2000,
there were three hundred seventy-four thousand Chinese
in New York City. Chinese American children don't seem
different from their classmates, who are increasingly from
many different races and countries.

Timeline

1949   June 27th, Vera Wang is born in New York City

1967   Vera graduates from the Chapin School in New York City and enters Sarah Lawrence College, Bronxville, New York.

1968   Vera and her partner, James Stuart, win the North Atlantic Contest for Junior Pairs Skaters.

1972   Vera graduates from Sarah Lawrence College and takes a job at Vogue Magazine.

1989   Vera marries Arthur Becker in the Pierre Hotel, New York City.

1990   Vera opens her own bridal shop in New York City.

1994   Vera designs a skating dress for Nancy Kerrigan, American Olympic Skater.

1998   Actress Sharon Stone, nominated for Best Actress, attends the Oscars wearing Vera Wang.

2005   Vera Wang is chosen Womenswear Fashion Designer of the Year.

Further Reading

Bryan, Nichol
Chinese Americans: One Nation, Set II
Edina, MN: ABDO, 2004.

Hoobler, Dorothy and Hoobler, Thomas
The Chinese American Family Album: The American Family Albums
New York, NY: Oxford University Press – USA, 1998.

Sills, Leslie
From Rags to Riches: A History of Girls' Clothing in America
New York: Holiday House, 2005.

Wang, Vera
Vera Wang on Weddings
New York: HarperCollins, 2001.

Websites

dragoneagle.com
is the website of the publisher of this book. On this site, you can find other books about Asians in America.

moca-nyc.org
is the website of the Museum of the Chinese in the Americas. Learn about Chinese American history on their resource page. Find out how to visit their museum in New York's Chinatown.

verawang.com
is Vera's official website. It contains photos of some of her latest designs.

Biographies of Amazing Asian Americans

J B WANG
Louie, Ai-Ling.
Vera Wang, queen of fashion :

To purchase copies of
Vera Wang, Queen of Fashion:
Amazing Chinese American
or copies of titles in
our forthcoming series,
Biographies of Amazing
Asian Americans,

visit our website:
dragoneagle.com.
or your local bookstore.

Coming next in our
biography series:
Yo-Yo Ma and Yeou-Cheng Ma,
Music and Medicine